Ice on the Move

Heather Hammonds

Contents

Rigby

Ice on the Move

Long ago, the earth was much colder. There was lots of ice.

Ice has helped to shape the earth.

Ice on the move is very **powerful**.

Today, we can see where ice has made **valleys** and shaped mountains.

Ice made this valley.

Glaciers

Glaciers are huge rivers of moving ice. They are found in very cold parts of the world.

Glaciers slowly move across the land.
Sometimes they reach the sea.
They become icebergs.

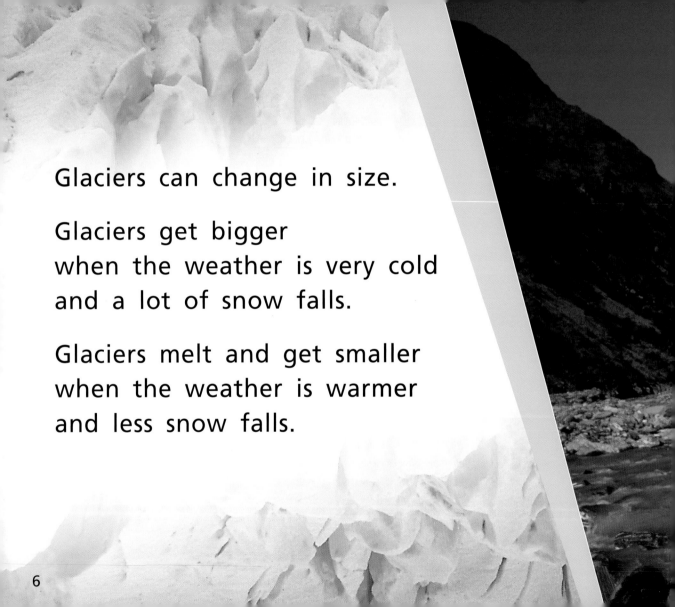

Glaciers can change in size.

Glaciers get bigger
when the weather is very cold
and a lot of snow falls.

Glaciers melt and get smaller
when the weather is warmer
and less snow falls.

This glacier changes in size
when the weather is hot or cold.

An Alpine Glacier

An alpine glacier grows between mountains. Snow falls at the top of the glacier and turns into ice. The glacier grows and grows.

Over a long time, the alpine glacier
moves slowly down the valley.
At the bottom of the valley,
it melts or breaks off into a lake
or the sea.

When Glaciers Move

Glaciers sometimes carry big rocks and dirt with them when they move.

Sometimes glaciers crack as they move. These cracks in glaciers are called **crevasses**.

Icebergs

When a glacier
reaches the sea
or a lake, big pieces
of ice break off.
Icebergs are formed.

Some icebergs are flat.

Some icebergs are **jagged**.

13

Only a small part
of an iceberg sits
above the water.
The rest of the iceberg
is below the water.

Icebergs can be a danger to ships.

In 1912, a ship called *Titanic* hit an iceberg and sank.

Today, ships use special **technology** to show them where the icebergs are.

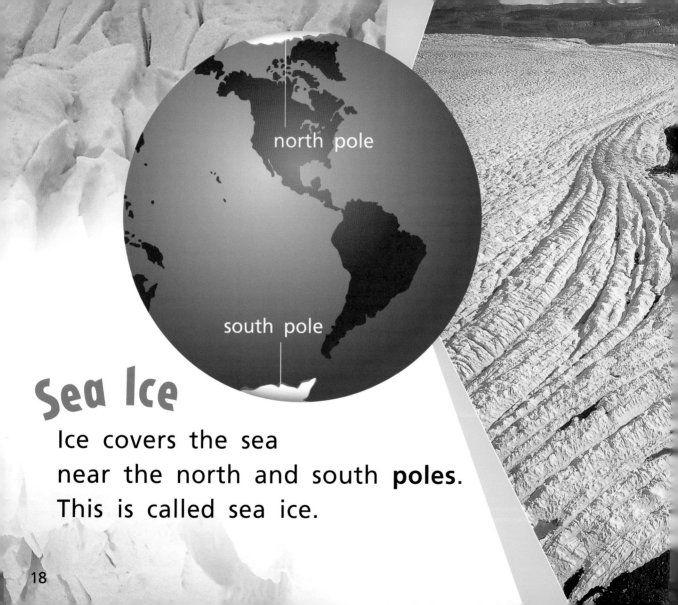

north pole

south pole

Sea Ice

Ice covers the sea
near the north and south **poles**.
This is called sea ice.

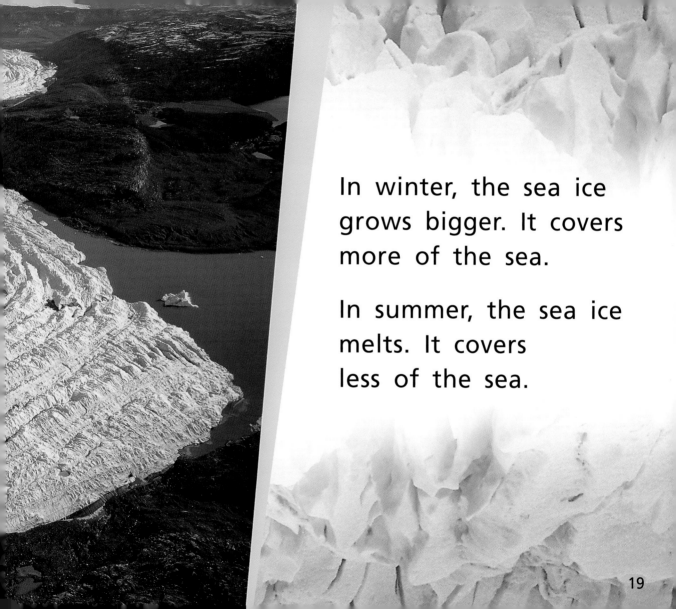

In winter, the sea ice grows bigger. It covers more of the sea.

In summer, the sea ice melts. It covers less of the sea.

Special ships
called **icebreakers**
cut through sea ice.
This helps other ships
get through the ice.

north pole

Greenland

Greenland

Greenland is a large island
near the north pole. Most of Greenland
is covered with ice.

Greenland has glaciers and icebergs.
In winter, sea ice forms around Greenland.

Antarctica

Antarctica is a **continent** at the south pole. Most of Antarctica is also covered with ice.

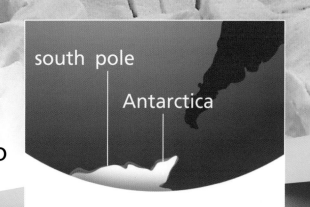

south pole

Antarctica

Antarctica has glaciers and icebergs, too. In winter, sea ice also forms around Antarctica.

Glossary

continent a big piece of land

crevasses big cracks in glaciers

icebreakers ships that cut through sea ice

jagged having many sharp bits that stick out

poles areas of land at the top and bottom of Earth

powerful very strong

technology special tools used to solve problems and get things done

valleys low areas of land between mountains and hills

Index